MUNKI TALES

MUNKI TALES

by Krissi Super

Mill City Press
212 3rd Ave N, Suite 290
Minneapolis, MN 55401
1-888-MILL CITY
www.millcitypress.net

ISBN 13: 978-1-936400-51-5
ISBN 10: 1-936400-51-0
LCCN: 2010935994

Printed in the United States of America
Book design by Wendy Arakawa

MUNKI'S DEDICATION

Throughout the past few years, some of the pets from our family have passed away and are no longer with us. I don't want to tell you all the heartbreaking stories, because it makes me depressed and sad. But it was, *like*, splendid that they all got to be part of our family for the time that they did. Each of them has found a permanent place in all our hearts. This book is dedicated to them and all the joy and love that they brought into our lives.

Cohin
Ezzi
Jimi
Poki
Uggils

HELLO

Welcome to my first book! I'm so happy that you are reading it! I'd first like to introduce myself, so you, *like*, know a little about me! My name is Valli Girl. I am a **Siamese** cat mixed with a little **Balinese**. That is my **breed** or what type of cat I am. There are tons of different breeds of cat, but personally, between you and me, I'm the coolest type of cat out there. Please don't tell my **tabby** sister Hiline I said that, because she'll get mad. More about her later.

I have to tell you about my favorite things. First of all, I love the color pink! Everything I own is pink: my fashionable collars, my fur brush, my traveling bag and crate, my fuzzy blanket, my food dishes, and my Hello Kitty collection. The cat room at my house is all decked out in pink, too. It's outta sight! When we got boy cats, I decided that we could add some blue. There's, *like*, definitely more pink, though. I like to look pretty all the time, so I dip my paws in water to clean them. During the day, I have to get my beauty sleep, so I take about three naps. I like looking at birds through the window and I make a funny little chirping sound when I see them. I like to snack on cat food and drink water out of a plastic cup. I don't drink water out of a bowl like other cats. That's just not the Valli Girl style!

My name comes from the 1960's, which is the decade my mommi has loved since she was a little girl. She digs the music, fashion, and lingo, and girls that lived in the San Fernando Valley in California during that time used the word *"like"* a lot. They were called Valley Girls. My mommi talks like that sometimes and so do I, so that's how I got my groovy name! By the way, I know that mommi is supposed to be spelled with a "y" at the end. But *my* mommi likes ending names with the letter "i" because her name, Krissi, does. That's the special way of spelling some of the names in our family.

You're probably wondering how a cat like me could write a book, right? Well, here's the deal. I didn't actually *write* the book, but I told it to my mommi, and she wrote it down for me! Because I'm part Siamese, I was born ready to talk. I talk all the time- just ask my mommi. I'm always like, "Mah, Mah, Mah!" I decided to tell this story, because I'm the only animal in my family that wasn't rescued, so I have a different point of view than them. I have seen how caring my parents have been to animals and what I have to say about **compassion** is, *like*, really important for people to learn about.

My life started out excellent. I was born on a farm by a sweet lady that raises cats like me. I was the last kitten left in the litter and nobody had picked me yet. I couldn't understand why not, because I was the cutest one! That's when my mommi found out about me. She already had one cat, but *like*, after seeing my picture and meeting me, she decided that she couldn't resist me. She adopted me and that's when my life as Valli Girl began.

So if my name is Valli Girl, then why is this book called *Munki Tales?* Well, Munki is the nickname that Jeremy gave me when I was a fuzzy little kitten. He thought I looked like a **meerkat** from the Animal Planet channel, which kind of looks like a monkey. Jeremy was my mommi's boyfriend when I was little and now they are married, so now he's my daddi! I'm quite sure that I'm his favorite, because when he asked my mommi to marry him, he put the shiny engagement ring on my pink collar. It was so cool!

I know I keep rambling on about myself and my life, but I, *like*, just have so many things that I want to tell you! I'm writing this book because I want every other cat and all other animals to have the same fabulous life as me. There are many **domestic animals** in the world that do not have homes and are treated very badly by people. I hope that when people read my book, they will learn how to be nice to animals and tell other people to be nice to them. I think the world would be a much better place if everybody were kind to all the animals, because we are very special creatures and all we want to do is make human beings happy!

I was one of the lucky ones. I was never abused or without a home and my life has always been a blast. Ever since I was born, I've had everything that I ever wanted and needed: food, water, shelter, and love. But not all animals are like me. There are many cats and dogs that don't, *like*, have anything. They're all alone in the world with nothing. There are also some very mean people that hurt animals and don't take care of them. I hope that my book will help stop some of the bad things that happen. I want to do all I can to rally around other animals, just like my mommi and daddi have. They have helped and adopted some of those animals in need of rescue.

Here are their tales...I hope you enjoy them!

Oh, by the way- all the blue words are animal-related terms I thought you should learn about. You can find their definitions in the back of the book in the Munki's Meanings section, along with some charming real-life pictures of some of the animals in this book!

TALE 1

HILINE

(HELENE)

HILINE

Hiline was my mommi's first cat. She adopted Hiline from her cousin's farm. She was born long before me, but we actually don't even know how old she is. A family couldn't have pets in their new house, so they dropped her off at the farm to live, but she was miserable there. She was used to, *like*, being inside all the time where it was cozy and warm, so mommi decided to save her from the cold! She was the first pet that mommi had since she lived on her own, so she was so excited to adopt her. She had to buy loads of fun supplies so Hiline had everything she needed when she moved in with her.

Hiline lived with my mommi for about two years before she adopted me. When I met Hiline for the first time, my little blue eyes grew very big. She was a fat, gray tabby cat and she had six toes on each paw! I was very afraid of her right away, because I was just a little kitten and she was *so* big. We had to be in separate rooms for the first week because she kept trying to fight with me. I tried to be really nice to her and said, "Hi! My name is Munki. I am, *like*, so happy to meet you and live here with you. Would you like to hang out and play?" But she didn't even look at me, she just hissed and walked away.

I understood why she was like that. She had been my mommi's only cat and then I came into the picture. She now had to share her food with me and she didn't like that very much. She wanted to eat it all herself! After a while, though, Hiline and I finally started to get along. I was getting bigger and smarter, so I knew when she wanted to be left alone or if she wanted to hang out with me. We would play with toys and sometimes we would take naps in the big, round cushion chair together. We formed a really special bond and mommi started to call us the "pretties." Having a new sister was the most!

TIP OF THE TALE

PET CARE

When you get a pet, be sure you supply everything they need to live a safe and happy life. For cats, you need items such as food and water dishes, cat food, treats, collars, ID tags, toys, beds, litter boxes, litter, and veterinary care. Dogs need many of those same things, except for the litter box, of course! The more you can give your pet, the more pleased they are. There are so many great items available for pets so shopping can be very fun. You will spoil them rotten!

THANK YOU FOR LISTENING TO MY ADVICE!

TALE 2
INKI

INKI

Hiline and I lived in an apartment with my mommi for a year before we moved to a new cabin by a lake. It was so cool, because I had a grand view of the pretty trees and water when I would perch in the window. The fresh breeze would come through the window screen and it was, *like*, so peaceful. It was just the three of us in the little cabin, until the day that mommi came home with a new addition to join us.

My mommi was at the same farm that she got Hiline from when she noticed a little kitten following her everywhere she went. She was a black **domestic shorthair** and the tiniest kitten in the litter- her brothers and sisters were twice her size! My mommi was worried about her surviving during the winter months, because it would be too cold for her to live outside, so she decided to take her home. When I first met her, I said, "Hi! My name is Munki. When I first saw you, I thought you were, *like*, a large, black mouse! You seem too small to be a cat!" I wasn't trying to be mean, I just couldn't believe it!

We named her Inki because, *well*...she looked like a blot of ink! She had been used to living outside and sleeping in a barn, so she had to adjust to her new life inside. It didn't take her long to find ways to have fun, though! She liked to wrestle with the little toy mice and her favorite thing to do was to nap on a bed by the fireplace. She loved the toasty heat on her fur and was so cozy and warm and happy. Hiline and I had a brand new sister and we were thrilled!

TIP OF THE TALE

INDOOR-OUTDOOR PETS

Pets want to be part of your family, so you should have them live inside with you. They like to be around people and need human interaction in order to be happy. If you have a pet that spends most of their time outside, though, *please* be sure they still get food and water and have a safe place to live and sleep, especially during extreme heat and cold. But remember: Outdoor pets don't live as long, because there are many dangerous things that can happen to them. Pets aren't objects, but rather members of your family, so let them live inside with you!

THANK YOU FOR LISTENING TO MY ADVICE!

TALE 3
EZZI,
BILLI JO,
PEARLI

EZZI, BILLI JO, PEARLI

One afternoon, I was gazing out the window and *suddenly*, I saw three big dogs digging through the garbage can! They looked dirty and hungry, so I figured they must have been lost. I yelled at them, "Hi! My name is Munki! Hang around until my mommi gets home from work, because she will, *like*, feed you and take care of you. Please stay!" So, of course they stayed. And of course, my mommi helped them! She gave them food and water and let them sleep inside by the fireplace. We worked hard to find their homes, but until we did, they continued to stay with us. During the day they hung out on the dock by the lake and at night they came inside the cabin to sleep. It seemed like they didn't have any other place to go.

We called places to see if anybody had reported the dog clan missing, but no luck. We tried so hard to find their homes, but nothing worked for us. We eventually decided the dogs must be **strays**, because they didn't have homes. That made me sad, because I, *like*, could not imagine being all alone and not having anyone to take care of me. Can you imagine that? We felt bad they didn't have a place to call home, so we kept the dogs for about two months and even named them.

We really liked all of them, but didn't have enough room to keep each one. Billi Jo, a female **German Shepherd**, and Pearli, a female **Boxer**, went to a **Humane Society** to stay until they found homes. We kept the last one- named Ezzi. She was a white and gray **Siberian Husky** mix and loved the cold Minnesota weather. During the winter, she loved to run on the frozen lake by the cabin and visit the people ice fishing. They would feed her treats and pet her soft fur. She was a funny dog that howled all the time and liked to play with all of us cats!

TIP OF THE TALE

LOST & FOUND

Sometimes pets get lost or run away from their homes and can't find their way back. That's why you should always have an I.D. tag on your pet or insert a microchip in them, because that will make it possible for you to track them down if they get lost. If you *find* a lost pet, you should always try to find its home first. You may want to keep the animal, but he or she might belong to someone else and they may be sad because they can't find their precious pet. If the animal doesn't have an I.D. tag, there are other ways to find the owner, such as placing a "FOUND" ad in the newspaper. Help the pet find their home and the family find their pet. It's the right thing to do.

THANK YOU FOR LISTENING TO MY ADVICE!

TALE 4
COHIN

COHIN

We had a full house at this point, but we definitely had love and compassion for more! Mommi was a teacher and people knew about her love for animals, so it wasn't a surprise when a co-worker told her about a stray cat that needed a home. The family that found him struggled to find him a place to live and they couldn't keep him any longer. Jeremy decided to go see him one day and sure enough, the cat was sitting outside by the doghouse. He looked very lonely, so he picked him up and took him to the cabin. When he walked in with him, I couldn't believe my eyes. I exclaimed, "Oh my goodness! You are a Siamese cat like me! By the way, my name is Munki and it's, *like*, really nice to meet you." I was completely shocked!

Because he had been a stray cat, he had to go to the veterinarian and get his shots to make sure that he was healthy. All of the animals in our house had to do that. It's important to do so nobody gets sick or has bad diseases. Once we knew he was well, Cohin got to move into the cabin with us. He was a little shy right away, because he was surrounded by all of us girl animals!

I didn't really like him at first because he was the first boy pet in the house and his attitude annoyed me. He, *like*, thought he was such a stud and strutted all over the cabin. He always wanted to go play outside, which was fine with me, because then I could take my beauty naps in peace. He would hang out in the woods during the day and I would watch him from my window chasing after mice and climbing trees. He looked like he was having fun, but he would always come in at night to sleep in the warm cabin. We got used to him and he ended up to be a great big brother to me, Hiline, Inki, and Ezzi.

TIP OF THE TALE

SPAY & NEUTER

Baby animals are obviously very cute and adorable, but there are too many of them being born that can't find homes. That's why you have to bring your pets to the veterinary hospital to **spay** and **neuter** them, so they don't continue to have litters of animals. Not only does spaying and neutering help keep the pet population down, but it also keeps your pet healthier and happier. There are millions of animals in the world that end up at shelters or on the streets, because too many pet owners don't spay and neuter. People need to be more responsible and take care of these issues!

THANK YOU FOR LISTENING TO MY ADVICE!

TALE 5
LINDI, UGGILS, MAX

LINDI, UGGILS, MAX

Sometimes people are allergic to animals and can't keep them anymore. This is what happened with Lindi. Mommi had a student and her mom got really sick when she was around her cat, so mommi took her in. Lindi, a white and black shorthair, also had something wrong with her eye, so we had to take extra good care of her. I think she was homesick after leaving her old house, but she got to bring her cat tower with to make her feel more comfortable. She was used to sleeping in it, playing on it, and scratching the posts. It looked so cool, so I said to her, "Hi! My name is Munki. Could I, *like*, play on your tower with you? I've never played on one before and it looks like so much fun!" She was nice enough to let me and the other cats play on it and it was so exciting!

After we got Lindi, we noticed that she was getting fatter. We soon realized that she was pregnant! She had four baby kittens on my mommi and daddi's wedding day! We found homes for the two Siamese mix kittens, but still had two black and white kittens left. We decided to keep Uggils- he had black and white spots on his face and was kind of funny looking. We felt bad for him right away, but soon realized he was really cool and didn't care how he looked. He had many different nicknames, like Uggs, Pugs, Pug-alicious, Mr. Delicious, and The Delicious One. He was, *like*, a pretty sweet dude and he could also fetch like a dog! Jeremy would throw his little furry mouse toy anywhere and he would bring it back to him in his mouth. We were all so jealous that he could do that, because we couldn't do anything that awesome.

To be responsible, we got Lindi spayed so she wouldn't have any more kittens in the future. Then my mommi convinced her brother to adopt both Lindi and the other black and white kitten, which he named Max. We were sad when they left, but we knew they would have a great home and he would take such good care of them. It was a happy ending for everybody. Hooray!

TIP OF THE TALE

FINDING HOMES

When you have a pet, things may happen when you might think you can't keep them anymore. Don't give away a pet because of behavior issues or because you just don't think it's working. Give it your best shot and do all you can to keep the pet in your family. Animals don't like to be shuffled from home to home, because it can be very stressful. If you absolutely have to give them up, be smart about your choices. If an animal is used to living inside, they cannot be put outdoors and know how to survive. If you can't find family or friends to adopt the pet, you can put an ad in the newspaper or place the pet on a website. Do your best to find a home they will like and adapt to and make sure their new family will love them.

THANK YOU FOR LISTENING TO MY ADVICE!

TALE 6 SUMMIR & CHINO

SUMMIR & CHINO

At the end of the school year, one of my mommi's students and his girlfriend were driving on a highway and saw two little kittens in the middle of the busy road. One was a gray tabby girl and the other was a fluffy orange tabby boy. They must have been deserted by someone, because they were huddled up together and very frightened. He took care of them as long as he could, but couldn't afford to keep them any longer, so he asked my mommi if she could take them. What do you think she said? Yes, of course!

She thought it was so cool that her student was concerned about the kittens, because a lot of young kids can be very mean to animals. My mommi heard some really bad stories in school, about kids abusing and killing animals, and that made her really sad and mad. Even though the boy that found the kittens loved animals, some of his friends were cruel to them. She knew that if she didn't take these kittens that something, *like*, really bad might happen to them.

She named the orange cat Chino and the gray cat Summir, after one of her favorite TV shows. They were so cute, but they were dirty so Jeremy had to give them many baths to clean them. They also had fleas so they had to wear special collars and took medicine to get rid of them. They were very afraid of everything right away, but once they got to our house, they had the best life ever! I said to them, "Hi! My name is Munki. The other cats don't think you are related, but I, *like*, know you are because you have identical eyes. You are definitely brother and sister!" They were always together and took care of each other. It was really special!

TIP OF THE TALE

STRAY ANIMALS

Remember- stray animals run loose and don't have anyone taking care of them. Because of that, if you ever find one that is hurt or helpless, you first need to be cautious. You may want to go pick them up and help them right away, but sometimes that can be dangerous. The animal might be sick or have fleas, so you need to get them checked out by a veterinarian first. If you don't, you might get ill from them if they bite you or other animals in your house might catch diseases. Once you know the animal is healthy, you can adopt them or find them a loving home!

THANK YOU FOR LISTENING TO MY ADVICE!

TALE 7
SALLI

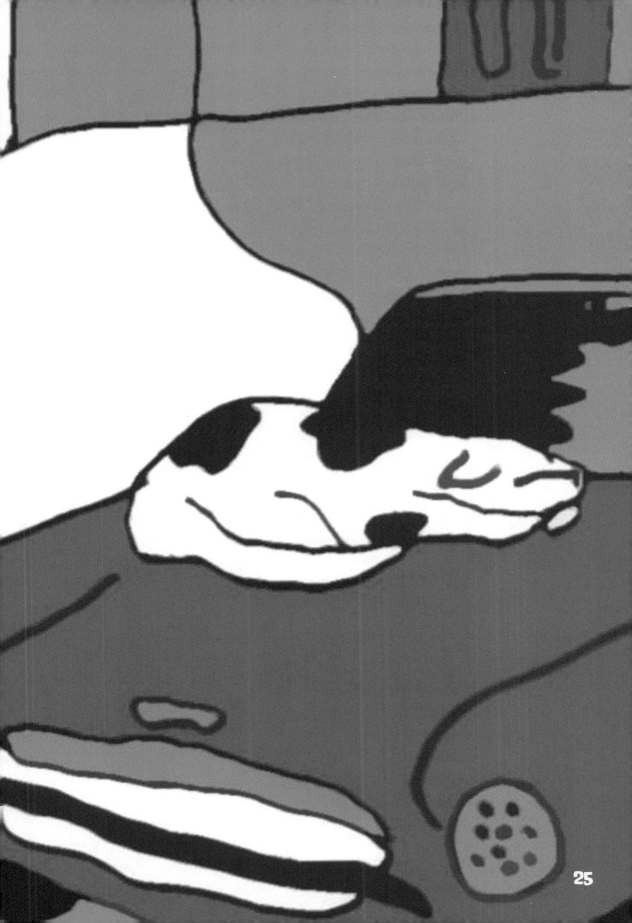

SALLI

It had been two years since my mommi adopted me and life was pretty awesome. I had grown up a lot and learned so many important things. My mommi and Jeremy were now married, so I could finally call him my daddi, which I was so excited about! We liked living in our new, big house with lots of room. I now had, *like*, ten different windows to gaze out of. It was so sweet!

One weekend, we went to my daddi's hometown to visit my grandparents. They were out in the workshop getting some tools, and all of a sudden, my daddi heard a squeaking noise. He searched all over and finally figured out what it was. There was a little kitten stuck underneath a Mustang convertible that was stored in the workshop. She had crawled up by one of the tires and gotten trapped, so daddi got on the dirty floor and tried to rescue her. My mommi was watching and was so scared because she thought the kitten might not make it. Luckily, though, he got her out safely and she survived! She must have been a stray cat that snuck in the workshop and got locked in. They couldn't believe that she was still alive, because she had eaten all of the rat poison in the shop. She was one tough little kitten.

Mommi and daddi decided to take her home because she needed a good place to live after being alone, scared, and hungry for so long. They named her Salli because she was saved from the Mustang and there is a song called "Mustang Sally". How funny is that?! She was a white domestic shorthaired cat with black spots on her back. When I met her, I said, "Hi! My name is Munki. I'm so happy daddi saved you, because you are a really nice cat. It must have been, *like*, very scary to be stuck under that car!" She said it was, but she was so happy she survived that cars didn't frighten her anymore. As a matter of fact, she started to take naps in the sunshine on the cars at our house. She did many things that were funny, so we started to call her Silli Salli!

TIP OF THE TALE

POISONS & HAZARDS

When you have a pet, be careful of poisons and toxins that they can access inside and outside of your house. Some animals get sick from things such as flowers, plants, cleaning supplies, chemicals, medication, and even certain foods. Make sure you keep all of those things away from your pet, because you want them to live a safe and happy life. If they do eat or swallow any of these items, be sure to call your veterinarian as soon as possible, so your pet can be saved. Also, when you leave your pet alone in your house, be certain there aren't places for your pet to get trapped in. Pets are smaller than people and very curious creatures, so they can get stuck in bad spots by accident.

THANK YOU FOR LISTENING TO MY ADVICE!

TALE 8
JIMI

JIMI

We had rescued many animals by this time, but we had a big house, so we all had our own space and life was just fantastic! One day, a friend of my mommi's told her that a dog showed up at her house. This dog was a black **Labrador Retriever** and it wouldn't leave her place. She fed him and took care of him, but she already had three other dogs and it wasn't possible for her to add one more. The weather was starting to get, *like*, really cold, so the dog couldn't keep sleeping outside. My mommi decided to take the dog and see if he would get along with Ezzi and then maybe we could keep him.

It was really sad that nobody had reported this dog missing. I said to him, "Hi! My name is Munki. You're such a handsome dog. Whoever let you go was, *like*, not a very smart person! Welcome to our family." We all figured he had been used for hunting and then once hunting season was over, the owners just dropped him off somewhere and left him. That happens a lot, especially where we live. People will come to the area and go duck, goose, and pheasant hunting and they'll buy dogs that will help retrieve the birds they shoot. When hunting season is over, they don't want the dogs anymore, so they just get rid of them. Some people will shoot and kill them and others will just leave them somewhere. This is the most ridiculous thing I've ever heard of. I can't believe that people can be this cruel and mean!

Anyway- we took in the dog and named him Jimi after one of mommi and daddi's favorite songs. He was a really nice dog, but hadn't been in a home for a long time, so he was just happy to have food, water, and a bed. He also got to go for cruises in the truck with my mommi, daddi, and Ezzi. He loved sticking his head out of the window in the fresh air, it made him so happy!

TIP OF THE TALE

RESPONSIBILITY

Before you get a pet, make sure that you and your family are ready to take care of them and understand how much work it is to raise them. You need to be very mature and dependable because there are many duties that go along with having a pet. You have to buy supplies, keep them healthy, and spend time with them. Some people get pets because they're cute, to protect their house, or for hunting, but then don't handle them properly. Make sure that the animal will have a loving home and will be treated well. Taking care of your pet also helps you become a better person, because it teaches you how to be responsible and compassionate!

THANK YOU FOR LISTENING TO MY ADVICE!

TALE 9
DAVI, HARMONI, MELODI
"THE CHRISTMAS CATS"

33

DAVI, HARMONI, MELODI

One of my favorite times of the year is Christmas. I love gazing at the pretty white snow outside and the fresh smell of cinnamon and evergreen. I love how my mommi decorates the house and hangs stockings for us animals. We get presents and treats and it's cozy in our warm home. One Christmas, Hiline, Ezzi, and I got to travel to my grandparents' house with my mommi and daddi. We were on our way home when all of a sudden, daddi turned his car around. We were in a separate car ahead of him with mommi and we didn't know what was happening. Then we realized that he saw three baby kittens in the middle of the road!

They were huddled together trying to stay warm in the cold winter weather. They got terrified when we got out of the car to rescue them so they ran into the ditch, but Ezzi sprinted down and rounded them up so we could catch them! When I first met them, I said, "Hi! My name is Munki. I'm happy we can help you! You can stay in my pretty pink crate because you need to be, *like*, really warm and safe." So mommi put the three kittens in my crate-they were so little that they all fit in one! We got them some food and water, because they were very small and skinny and cold.

We took them home with us, of course, and we decided to keep all three kittens after we couldn't find them decent places to live. The two girls were **tortoiseshell** cats and the boy was a gray domestic shorthair with big white whiskers. We named the twin girls Melodi and Harmoni, because they would always sing for their food in the morning. They sounded like chorus cats! We named the boy Davi, because that just seemed to be, *like*, the perfect name for him. We're pretty sure he's their brother, even though he doesn't look like them. They are very lucky that we found them that day and we feel the same way about them. At one time they didn't have a home on Christmas, but now they have their own stockings every year!

TIP OF THE TALE

ANIMAL CRUELTY

Leaving animals in the middle of a road is animal cruelty and it's against the law! If you neglect your pet and don't give them the proper care, you are abusing them. Domestic animals depend on humans to survive, and it's hard for them to live on their own without your help. Don't ever let animals suffer! Animal cruelty also includes beating, shooting, kicking, or stabbing an animal, and many people that are cruel to animals are also cruel to humans. So if you ever see someone being mean to animals, make sure you first tell them to stop and if they don't, tell somebody about it as soon as you can.

THANK YOU FOR LISTENING TO MY ADVICE!

TALE 10
POKI

POKI

By this time, my daddi was a teacher, and he was working in a different school than my mommi. One day another teacher told him about a cat that she had seen hanging around a casino she drove by each day. The cat had been in the same place outside for almost two weeks and he looked lost and afraid and didn't have anywhere to go. I can't believe that nobody else was worried about the cat, especially since there were so many people around that building each day. Some people just don't care about animals and it makes me so upset!

One day my daddi decided to rescue the cat from his loneliness. He picked up the long, skinny gray tabby and brought him home. He called mommi from his cell phone and told her he had a present for her. It was, *like*, going to be a surprise, but she heard the cat meow in the background! She couldn't believe he was bringing another cat into the mix, but she wasn't surprised either. They both enjoy doing whatever they can to help animals in need.

They named the cat Poki, short for Poker, because he was the casino cat. He mainly hung outside and chased after mice and rolled around in the grass, but he would sleep in the warm garage at night with Cohin. When I met him, I said, "Hi! My name is Munki. It looks like you're having fun playing outside. I would play with you, but I, *like*, need to be inside because that's where I've lived all my life and I don't want to get dirty." But he liked the outside life, because that's how he lived before we adopted him. Instead of being all alone, though, he now had a family to feed him, love him, and give him a safe place to live. He hit the jackpot with us!

TIP OF THE TALE

TRAINING YOUR PET

Animals can't scamper around wherever they want to, so you have to train them to stay at your house and know where they are at all times. There are laws you need to follow that say your pet must stay at their home and not roam around the neighborhood. You also need to train cats and dogs, so they go to the bathroom in the right places. Indoor cats use litter boxes and dogs need to go outside. It may take some time to train your pet, but it's very important and will keep your pet safe and happy.

THANK YOU FOR LISTENING TO MY ADVICE!

TALE 11
MORRISON

MORRISON

We now lived in a brand new house that my mommi and daddi bought and it was me, Hiline, Inki, Salli, Chino, Summir, Davi, Melodi, and Harmoni. Something special was, *like*, missing from the picture, though. I spoke up for the rest of the cats and told mommi and daddi that we would like to have a dog come live with us. Of course they listened to me, so they searched on Petfinder.com and found a dog named Frisbi. He was at a Humane Society shelter and they were so excited to go get him!

He was seven months old when they adopted him, and they decided to change his full name to Morrison Thielen, but his nickname soon turned to Morry. When I met him, I said, "Hi! My name is Munki. Just so you know, it was *my* idea to get you. I am, *like*, so happy you are finally here!" We figured he was a **mixed-breed** dog with some Husky and Labrador Retriever in him, but we weren't sure. It didn't matter what his breed was, because he was so cute and friendly! Every time he would go outside, he would eat the snow, because when he was a stray, he did that when he was thirsty. Now he had his own doggy bed in the house and got to play with all of us cats and his fun toys!

When the weather got nice outside, my mommi took him running in the morning and he loved all of the exercise. When they finished the trek, Morry was so tired and thirsty that he always drank a full bowl of water! It was great to have a dog in our family again, even though some of the cats were a little frightened of him right away. They soon realized he was a nice doggy and that he would always love and protect us.

TIP OF THE TALE

EXERCISE

It's very important for pets to get exercise. Cats like to move freely, jump for toys, and chase after objects. Dogs like to run around, fetch balls and sticks, and sometimes even swim. While you might have to keep your dog tied to a leash or in a kennel *some* of the time, you have to make sure it's not *all* of the time. That is not a nice way to treat animals, because they need freedom and human interaction. Can you imagine if you were in a kennel your whole life or tied to a tree? That would be a sad and lonely life. Give your pet a fun and joyful life!

THANK YOU FOR LISTENING TO MY ADVICE!

TALE 12

HUGHI

&

HURLI

HUGHI & HURLI

And now for the last tale of the dozen! It's about the most recent animals that joined our family. My mommi tried to find them homes, but it, *like*, just worked out that they fit in very well with the rest of us. They came from a home that couldn't keep them anymore and then my mommi's cousin took them from there and then my mommi got them from her and then my mommi gave them to someone who decided not to keep them, so then she took them back to our house. Can you keep up with all my crazy stories? I hope so!

When they first arrived at our house, they were very well-behaved and weren't shy around anybody, because they were used to being around plenty of different people and animals. They really liked to cuddle with mommi and daddi. I said, "Hi! My name is Munki. We all used to cuddle like that when we were young, but now we're, *like*, older and more independent so we don't do that as much." I actually might have been a little jealous, because they got so much attention right away.

We think they might be brother and sister, but they don't really look alike. They just act alike! Hughi is a **domestic longhair** with tan and white fur. His fur got so long that it matted up in knots, so mommi brought him to the pet groomer to get it shaved. Now he looks like a lion and he is so much happier! Hurli is a white, brown, and black **calico** cat that's very feisty. She has a little black smudge on her nose and likes to get into any kind of food she can. They like to play on the yarn chairs in our house and Hurli always sneaks up on Hughi. Hughi gets tricked every single time and can't figure out what she is doing! We're happy to have them in our house. Our Animal House, as we like to call it.

TIP OF THE TALE

CLEANLINESS

If you have an animal or lots of animals at our house, you need to make sure that you keep things clean. Not only is it nice to live in a home that smells fresh, but animals value neatness, too. Make sure you clean litter boxes, food dishes, collars, crates, and kennels. Clean your pet's teeth and ears and bathe them or bring them to a pet groomer to keep their fur silky, smooth, and smelling good! Sometimes pets make a mess at your house, so you should have cleaning supplies ready to clean it up. Keeping everything spotless makes life pleasant for the humans and the animals alike. You'll be one big happy family if you do!

THANK YOU FOR LISTENING TO MY ADVICE!

GOODBYE

Thank you so much for reading the tales! I really hope that you enjoyed them! I like the fact that all of the animals were rescued from bad situations and able to start a new, amazing life. My mommi and daddi showed their compassion and their willingness to make the animals' lives better in so many different ways. You know what's really sweet about that? Not only did they make the animals happier, but the animals, *like*, made them happier, too! Don't tell them I told you this, but I hear them talking about us all of the time and saying how much they love us. It seems like we bring a lot of joy into their lives. I think it's so awesome that we make them happy!

I think my parents are the best, because they've done so much to help so many animals, but they can't help them all. I hope that after you read this book, you will pass it on to someone else and then, with any luck, everybody will soon understand how important it is to love and watch over animals. We depend on you to live a safe and happy life, so it's very crucial that you help. And guess what? If you promise to help *us*, I promise we will lend a paw to *you*!

Animals can help assist people in many ways. Some are used as therapy animals, such as seeing-eye dogs, cancer sniffing dogs, and epilepsy and seizure sensing dogs, and help people with disabilities. There are some animals that live in nursing homes and hospitals and help elderly and sick people. Some dogs are trained by the police and help solve big-time crimes, and others are used in the military and help soldiers during wars. But most of all, above all else, animals make great companions.

We love being with you and want to make your life magnificent every day! We each do special things to make that happen. The more time you spend with us, the more you will find we are just as unique as you. Pets all have one-of-a-kind personalities and certain quirks that make them stand out from one another. It's important to keep us a big part of your life, so you can learn how special we really are!

*FAUX FEATHER BOA

Because we're so special, you should care for us the best you can. Taking care of cats and dogs and other pets teaches people how to be responsible and how to be considerate of another living thing. If you learn how to be kind to us animals, it will carry over to your kindness for your fellow humans. I hope one day that everybody- all animals and humans- will live in a world where there is no cruelty or meanness, but only peace, love, and compassion. It would be, *like,* the coolest thing ever!

MUNKI'S MEANINGS

Balinese
A Balinese cat is a longhaired version of the Siamese cat. Balinese cats are smart, sweet, and fun to be around. They are well-known for being talkative, social, and ready to make you happy with their cheerful chatter.

VALLI GIRL "MUNKI"

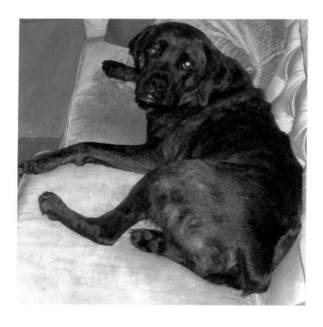

Boxer
A Boxer is a breed of dog that has a blend of strength, speed, and style. They have a square shape with a big, rounded muzzle, and strong muscles. They are playful, outgoing, and listen well. They are an ideal dog for an energetic family and are fine with other pets.

PEARLI (Tale #3)

breed
A certain rank for the organization of domestic cats and dogs.

calico
A coat pattern that combines the red and black patches of the tortoiseshell with patches of white.

HURLI (Tale #12)

compassion
Awareness of the suffering of others and showing a need to make it better. Compassion can be displayed towards both humans and animals.

domestic animals
Animals that are trained to live and breed in a tame condition.

domestic longhair
A domestic longhair is a mixed-breed cat. Domestic longhair cats have long, fluffy fur, and they need to be brushed often to avoid matted fur and hairballs. They come in a variety of colors, as well as many patterns, including tabby and solid. Domestic longhairs can have different body types and facial expressions.

HUGHI (Tale #12)

domestic shorthair

A domestic shorthair is a mixed-breed cat. Domestic shorthair cats have short, sleek fur, and only need to be brushed occasionally to get rid of loose fur. They come in a variety of colors, as well as many patterns, including tortoiseshell, tabby, and solid. Domestic shorthairs can have different body types and facial expressions.

INKI (Tale #2)

DAVI (Tale #9)

LINDI (Tale #5)

SALLI (Tale #7)

UGGILS (Tale #5)

MAX (Tale #5)

German Shepherd

The German Shepherd is one of the smartest of the dog breeds and they are protective of their home and family. While they are very faithful to their families, they might be a bit standoffish to strangers. The German Shepherd has a long body and they are very strong and have quick movements.

BILLI JO (Tale #3)

Humane Society

An organization that promotes kindness and compassion towards animals.

Labrador Retriever

Labrador Retrievers are active and sociable dogs. They come in different colors, such as black, brown, white, and yellow. They need exercise every day and love to run, retrieve and swim. They are able to live in outdoor climates, but they are happier indoors with their family. They are good with children and other dogs and pets.

JIMI (Tale #8)

meerkat

A type of mammal (mongoose) from southern Africa that is mainly grayish with faded black markings and lives in large colonies.

mixed-breed

An animal that has characteristics of two or more breed types.

MORRISON (Tale #11)

neuter

An operation a male animal has so that they can no longer reproduce.

Siamese

The Siamese is one of the oldest breeds of domestic cat. They have baby blue eyes, sleek fur, and like to talk. They have a talent for communicating their thoughts and requests to humans. They love to be involved in their families' life and need lots of love and affection.

COHIN (Tale #4)

Siberian Husky

The Husky is a fun-loving, daring, and stubborn dog. They love to run, howl, dig, and chew. They need lots of exercise and love cold weather. They can survive living outdoors, but would rather live indoors with their family, as long as they get enough time to run and play outside.

EZZI (Tale #3)

spay

An operation a female animal has so that they can no longer reproduce.

strays

Domestic animals that are wandering at large or are lost.

tabby

A coat pattern known for stripes and/or patches of color, like spots or blotches. Cats of this type have varying fur type and color.

HILINE (Tale #1)

CHINO & SUMMIR (Tale #6)

POKI (Tale #9)

tortoiseshell

A coat pattern with a mix of patched colors, found mainly in female cats. Cats of this type are speckled, with patches of orange, brown, black or blue.

MELODI (Tale #9)

HARMONI (Tale #9)

Some information retrieved from the following helpful websites:
http://animal.discovery.com
www.animalhumanesociety.org
www.animalshelter.org
www.catster.com
www.humanesociety.org
www.webster.com

FROM THE AUTHOR

These tales are all based on actual animal rescue stories from my life. To quote animal activist and country singer Emmy Lou Harris, *"Animals can teach us how to be better human beings."* They definitely have helped me to become a better person- more responsible and more compassionate. Although it is not always an easy job taking care of all the animals we have rescued, it definitely is always an easy choice to do so. My husband and I have never hesitated to help these animals, and we would help many more if we could. I have learned so much through the unconditional love from animals. They are not objects and we should not treat them like that. They are living beings and we need to make a more conscious effort to protect them and love them. I hope this book will help educate people both young and old and will raise awareness of many topics associated with defending animals.

Profits from this book will be used towards starting my own animal rescue business & awareness program.

—Krissi Super

CPSIA information can be obtained at www.ICGtesting.com
Printed in the USA
BVIW12n0912140818
524466BV00011B/88